I0522038

For more information contact the publisher at:
Patton Girl LLC
11582 SW village parkway
Unit # 157
Port saint Lucie FL 34987
Or email Pattongirl.LLC@gmail.com

THIS BOOK

BELONGS TO:

_____

INTRODUCTION

Have you ever caught yourself leaving work, only to find that your mind is still racing about everything that happened that day or what tasks you have to do for the next? Having a long to-do list when running a business is common, and it can be challenging to switch off those thoughts outside of work hours. However, achieving a work-life balance is crucial for your health and productivity. When you set aside time to disconnect from work, you allow your mind to recharge and reset, allowing you to be more productive when you return to it. So, why not make work-life balance a priority in your life? It could be the key to achieving greater success at work and home.

But if it were that easy, why haven't you perfected the perfect work-life balance already?

You understand the pivotal role that work plays in your life. It's not just about paying the bills and keeping food on the table. It's about having the ability to plan for the unexpected and live a comfortable life. But let's be honest - balancing work and life is a challenge. It can feel like we're constantly playing catch-up, with not enough time to enjoy the fruits of our labor truly. And let's not even get started on the added stress of rising energy bills and the cost-of-living crisis. But don't worry, you're not alone in this struggle.

As you sit at your kitchen table, laptop open, sipping on your morning coffee, you can't help but think about the blurred lines between work and personal life. This new way of working from home has become the norm for many, but it's starting to feel like there's no escape from the demands of your job. Checking emails outside the usual 9-to-5 workday has become commonplace, and taking calls during dinnertime has become the new normal. So the question remains: how did we get to this point where it's considered acceptable? It's time to step back and reevaluate the boundaries between work and personal life to ensure a healthier and happier balance.

In the wake of the pandemic, it seems that priorities have shifted when it comes to the workplace. According to a study by Aviva, work-life balance has become more important than salary to most workers. This marks a distinct change from 2019 when salary was ranked higher than work-life balance. Perhaps this sudden shift in priorities can be attributed to the rise of remote work and the newfound flexibility it has afforded employees. Whatever the cause, it's clear that more and more people recognize the value of striking a healthy work-life balance. After all, what good is a high salary if it comes at the cost of one's mental and physical well-being?

That's exactly what this eBook, **The Ultimate Work-Life Balance Checklist**, is for! But to understand why we wrote this eBook, it's essential to understand what work-life balance is and why it's crucial.

■ What is work-life balance?

You may have heard of the term "work-life balance" numerous times in your career, and you may even believe you have a solid grasp of its meaning. However, the truth is many of us have been misguided in our understanding of this concept. Work-life balance is often defined as devoting equal amounts of time to work and leisure activities. Still, this simplistic definition fails to consider our lives' complexity. Rather than focusing solely on time spent at work versus home, we need to understand the intricate interplay between our professional and personal lives. Only then can we begin to appreciate the importance of achieving a true work-life balance beyond clocking in and out daily.

You might think time management is the key to achieving a better work-life balance. After all, we're constantly bombarded with productivity hacks and flexible work schedules as the solution. However, the truth is that time is not the real problem here. The iconic see-saw image of balancing work and life is just a myth. The reality is that you can't simply manage your time better to achieve balance - it just doesn't work. Countless people have tried and failed. Instead, you must focus on other aspects of your life, like prioritizing your health and well-being, learning to say 'no' when necessary, and establishing clear boundaries between work and home. Remember, balance is not a finite concept - it's a mindset and a continual journey.

Have you ever wondered what a balanced lifestyle would look like for you? It's a concept many strive for, yet few achieve. When considering what this ideal balance entails, most people describe things like making a greater impact at work and in the world without sacrificing personal health and happiness, positively impacting their children's lives, and prioritizing self-care without guilt or shame. Another crucial aspect of balance is being present in the moment, with the mental space to fully process and enjoy life's experiences. Having solid boundaries that align with your values and letting go of the pressure to do or have it all can also play a significant role in nurturing a balanced lifestyle. Achieving balance is a lofty goal, but it is worth striving for and achievable.

When it comes to work-life balance, it's easy to fall into the trap of thinking that it's something you can find, like a lost pair of keys. But in reality, balance is something that you create for yourself through the choices you make. And at the heart of those choices is your mindset. Are you content with who you are and the decisions you're making? Are you willing to make tough choices in order to achieve the balance you seek? Ultimately, work-life balance isn't just about managing your time, it's about feeling fulfilled in all aspects of your life. So take control and start creating the balance that works best for you.

Have you ever found yourself feeling off-kilter like you're juggling too many balls at once? The concept of balance is easy to understand in theory, but what does it truly entail? Is it just about squeezing in a workout session once a week, or is there more to it? And in today's fast-paced world, where our personal and professional lives often collide, finding that elusive balance can seem like an unattainable goal. So how do we navigate the delicate dance of work and home while maintaining our sanity and inner peace?

◼ Why is finding a work-life balance necessary?

Creating a more balanced life can seem like a daunting task, but it's an important one. It requires you to prioritize what really matters and let go of the things that don't. It also requires taking control of your career path and simplifying your life. But it's not just about making tough choices. It's about having the courage, mental strength, and resilience to do so. In order to find this courage, your mind needs to understand why balance is so important. Then, when you fully buy into the why, you'll be inspired to act with conviction and make the necessary changes to lead a more balanced life.

Have you ever thought that work-life balance is only essential for women? Think again. Men value balance just as much as women, but they use different language. Women talk about balance and leading meaningful lives, while men talk about having time for their priorities and making an impact. However, at the core of these statements, both men and women say the same thing. They want a fulfilling life that includes time for work, family, and personal pursuits. So, let's make it clear - work-life balance is for everyone, regardless of gender.

So, how do you create a work-life balance that works for every aspect of your life?

Let's explore the art of balance together.

■ Chapter One: It Starts with Work Time

Finding a work-life balance that actually works for you can feel like an elusive concept. For example, you might have tried slicing up your day or week to give equal time to work and personal life, only to find that special projects invariably keep you in the office past 5 p.m. or that unforeseen circumstances arise in your personal life, like having to care for a sick child, that throws a wrench in your workday. But there is hope. Achieving a work-life balance means prioritizing the things that matter most to you and learning to be intentional with your time.

By focusing on the essential tasks and being flexible when the unexpected arises, you'll be on your way to finding the balance that's right for you.

Here are some tips for creating healthy work-life boundaries at work:

Use Your PTO

You work hard, but taking time for yourself is essential too. Don't fall victim to the statistic that 55% of American workers leave their paid vacation days unused. You deserve a break from the daily grind. Even if you're worried about returning to piles of work, it's time to let go of that excuse. It's crucial to have a healthy balance between work and time off. And that means disconnecting from your work phone and email while on vacation. Instead, sit on the beach, listen to the waves, and recharge your batteries. Then, when you return to work, you'll feel refreshed and ready to tackle challenges. So, go ahead and take that vacation. Your little piece of paradise is waiting for you.

Take Breaks During Your Day

You may have thought that working through your lunch hour and powering through your workday is the best way to get things done. However, research shows that your brain needs a break in order to stay productive.

DeskTime, a productivity app, found that the most efficient employees work for around 52 minutes, then take a 17-minute break. This short break allows your brain to recuperate and recharge, allowing you to come back with a fresh perspective and renewed energy. Not to mention, anticipating a break can motivate you to remain focused and engaged during your work time. You might be surprised at how much more efficient you'll become by giving yourself a chance to recharge your batteries.

■ Create Physical Boundaries

When working from home, it's essential to establish boundaries between your workspace and your personal space. It can be tempting to set up shop in convenient locations, like your bed or kitchen table, but resist the urge! Instead, you need to create a dedicated workspace to help you focus on work and avoid distractions. For example, consider transforming a guest room or enclosed porch into a cozy and comfortable office space. Or, if you're tight on space, turn your large laundry room, garden shed, or walk-in closet into a productivity haven. Whatever you do, ensure your workspace is separate from your personal space. By establishing these boundaries, you'll be able to be more productive in your work-from-home routine.

Find the Right Culture

It can be incredibly frustrating when you feel like your efforts to please everyone at work are not paying off. Your attempts to communicate the importance of work-life balance may feel like they're falling on deaf ears, leaving you feeling stuck in a dead-end job. But don't despair - there are plenty of options out there that will allow you to find a better work-life balance. Whether it's a job with a flexible schedule, a remote workplace, or a company culture that truly values its employees, there is a path forward that will help you get the rest and recharge time you need. So don't be afraid to take the leap and find a job that respects your boundaries and supports your well-being. Your mental health and happiness are worth it!

Disconnect when you're home.

Do you ever feel like you can never fully disconnect from work or the outside world? Getting caught up in the constant notifications and alerts from texts, emails, and calls is easy. But have you ever stopped to consider how this affects your well-being? Stress levels can skyrocket when we feel we need to be available 24/7. And constantly checking your phone distracts you from connecting with loved ones and can also negatively impact your sleep. It may be difficult, but try turning off or muting your phone or even leaving it in another room when spending time with family or winding down for the day. Remember, taking care of yourself is just as, if not more, important than being available at all times.

■ Prioritize self-care

You are busy, constantly juggling work, family, and personal life. It's easy to prioritize everything else above our health and well-being. But it's time to decide - set aside time for exercise, choose and plan nutritious meals, and carve out quality time for friends and family. Make these things non-negotiable in your schedule. Remember, self-care isn't a luxury - it's a necessity. By prioritizing your physical and mental health, you'll be more energized, focused, and happy.

■ Chapter Two: Next, It's All About Family Time

Are you finding it a challenge to juggle your work and family commitments? You are not alone. With the pressure to meet deadlines and excel at work coupled with the need to give your family the attention they need, it is no wonder that stress levels are on the rise. However, it is essential to strike a balance between the two, as neglecting one for the other could lead to negative consequences. To achieve this balance, you might need to set boundaries at work and prioritize spending quality time with your loved ones. Remember, your well-being and that of your family should always come first.

So how do you keep your work separate from your family and prioritize family time as needed to find the perfect balance?

Let's find out!

Remove Stress

Maintaining a sense of clarity and inner peace can feel like an elusive goal when the demands of daily life pile up. The constant grind can leave you feeling drained and weighed down by stress hormones, inhibiting your ability to perform at your best. But fear not, friend- there are ways to recalibrate and find balance within your busy schedule. For example, indulging in activities that help to lower your stress levels, such as meditation or mindfulness exercises, can help to clear your mind and relax your body, allowing you to return to your work and your loved ones with renewed vigor and a sense of calm. So take a deep breath, make time for yourself, and prioritize your well-being- you and those around you will reap the benefits.

Focus On Family Time

You're busy, and life can sometimes feel like a never-ending to-do list. But when it comes to your family, it's essential to set aside time devoted entirely to them. You can't just wait for a break in your schedule to appear magically. Instead, gather the family together and make a plan. First, ensure everybody is on the same page about the importance of time spent together. Then, work together to outline the steps you need to take to ensure it happens. This could mean scheduling in-person visits, setting up regular phone calls with family members who live far away, or planning special activities to enjoy together. Whatever approach you take, make sure you all stay committed to the goal of spending time together. After all, family is the most important thing of all.

Strengthen Your Bond with Family

Building strong communication with your loved ones is crucial to balancing work and family. Sharing your work struggles with your family members helps them understand the challenges you face daily, making them more supportive and less demanding. In addition, when you communicate openly and honestly, your family members feel heard and respected, leading to better reactions when prioritizing work over family. Remember, open communication is a two-way street, so make sure you also listen to your family members' concerns and issues. By fostering solid familial bonds, you create a foundation of trust, understanding, and support that can help you easily manage work and family life.

Develop A Routine

Balancing your family and work life is daunting, but it all comes down to consistency. Being consistent doesn't mean cutting corners or skimping on vital tasks. Instead, it means creating a routine for yourself that allows you to unwind and relax at the end of the day. Building a schedule that suits your needs will help you avoid burnout and ensure you use your time efficiently. Remember, it's not about working yourself into the ground. It's about finding a healthy and sustainable balance that will enable you to succeed in your career and personal life. So take charge, create a plan, and stick to it, and you'll be amazed at how much easier juggling work and family responsibilities can be.

Developing a routine can seem daunting, but it can be a game changer for your work and family life. Setting a schedule for yourself can increase your consistency and focus, allowing you to spend more quality time with loved ones. For example, if you're an early riser, take advantage of those quiet morning hours to finish some tasks before the kids wake up. This can give you a head start on your day and allow for a relaxed breakfast with your family. Likewise, if your kids have after-school activities, pack dinner for a post-game picnic. By finding a routine that works for you and your family, you can be on your way to a more organized and fulfilling lifestyle.

As you navigate the demands of daily life, it's essential to take the time to create unforgettable memories with your loved ones. Whether exploring a new city, cooking dinner together, or settling in for a cozy night at home, these moments will become precious touchstones in your family's shared history. To balance family life, you must prioritize and build these experiences into your routine. Even with busy schedules and competing demands, carving out time for quality moments together will help you strengthen your relationships and create happy memories that last a lifetime.

Chapter Three: Hanging Out With Your Friends

As you navigate the demands of work, family, and everyday life, it's easy to let friendships fall by the wayside. However, developing and maintaining a network of supportive friends is critical to achieving a healthy work-life balance. Studies show that individuals with strong friendships experience better mental health, lower stress levels, and a stronger immune system. But friendships aren't formed overnight and require ongoing nurturing to endure. Whether it's scheduling regular get-togethers, checking in on your friends, or being open to new connections, taking intentional steps to prioritize social connection will profoundly impact your overall well-being. So why not invest in yourself and build long-lasting friendships today?

What are the benefits of making time for friends?

Having good friends in your life is enjoyable and essential for your overall well-being. As you navigate life's ups and downs, having a supportive and caring group of friends can make all the difference. Celebrating the good times with friends creates cherished memories, and having them by your side during tough times can help you cope and feel less alone. However, it's important to remember that friendship is a two-way street, and it's equally important to offer support to your friends when they need it. So, cherish your friendships and make time to nurture these relationships- your health depends on it!

When life gets busy, it's easy to let connection with friends fall by the wayside. However, intentionally making time for those close to you can result in many benefits. Not only can it increase your sense of belonging and purpose, but it can also boost happiness and reduce stress levels. It may even improve your self-confidence and self-worth. Moreover, during times of hardship, having a solid support system of close friends can be invaluable for coping with traumas.

Additionally, spending time with friends can encourage you to make healthier choices and avoid harmful habits. Prioritizing friendships may seem like another item on the to-do list, but the rewards are worth the effort. Take a moment to reach out to a friend and make plans - your mental and physical health will thank you.

Having friends is not just about having someone to spend time with. It's also about having a positive impact on your health. Studies have shown that people with strong social connections tend to have better health overall, including lower risks of depression, high blood pressure, and an unhealthy BMI. In addition, as you get older, having meaningful relationships and social support becomes even more critical. Older adults with a network of supportive friends are likely to live longer than those with few connections. So, don't underestimate the power of friendship - it's more than just a good time. It's a vital part of your overall well-being.

■ Why It's Important To Make Time For Social Activities

You know that feeling you get when you're surrounded by people who love and support you? That warm, fuzzy feeling that makes everything seem a little brighter? Well, it turns out that feeling isn't just in your head. According to Dr. Dana Avey (Licensed Marriage and Family Therapist, Certified Psychiatric Rehabilitation Practitioner, Certified Holistic Life Coach, and Distance Credentialed Counselor), spending time with friends and family can significantly impact your mental health and overall well-being. Not only does socializing improve your mood at the moment, but the benefits continue long after the hangout session is over. So, next time you're feeling down or stressed, don't underestimate the power of an excellent ol' fashioned chinwag with someone you care about. Your mind (and heart) will thank you for it.

Having a positive group of peers is essential to your mental and emotional well-being. It's easy to become trapped in your thoughts and struggles, but connecting with others who can offer objective feedback and support is just as important as physically caring for yourself. Engaging with others also has many benefits beyond those, such as inspiration and motivation, building self-esteem, teaching empathy and acceptance, creating a sense of value within yourself, reinforcing a sense of identity, increasing your perception of meaning, and even decreasing stress levels. Joining or building a supportive community of peers can have an incredibly positive impact on your life.

You may be surprised to learn that having a positive social network can actually add years to your life. It turns out that socializing isn't just good for your emotional well-being. It's good for your physical health too. And who doesn't want to live a longer, healthier life? Feeling better physically can also positively impact your mental and emotional state, helping you live a more fulfilling life overall. So don't be shy about reaching out and making connections with others. If you're unsure where to start, we've got some helpful tips to help you build your social network today. So what are you waiting for? It's time to get out there and start socializing!

So what can you do?

Identify Priority People

Prioritize the people you want to make time for. Decide who to fit into your schedule based on their importance, not because of any familial ties. These can include family, close friends, and those with whom interactions are motivating and inspiring. Don't forget to use the extra time to connect with those who didn't make the list!

Be Sure To Make Time For You

Balance is essential - schedule time for yourself to relax, reflect and recharge. Setting aside personal time ensures you can always give others your best self. Add activities like exercise, meditation, financial planning, self-reflection, reading, or gardening to your calendar for energized interactions with those around you. Taking care of yourself first can avoid social and volunteer overload.

Finding a good work-life balance can be elusive in today's always-on culture. But don't lose hope just yet – some strategies can help you reclaim some balance. One approach might be to embrace technology in a new way. Instead of fighting it, use it to your advantage. With intelligent scheduling tools and remote work options, you can be just as productive from home as in the office. The key is to set boundaries and stick to them. Designate specific times for work and play, and honor those commitments. By taking a proactive approach, you can create a fulfilling personal and professional life supporting your well-being.

When it comes to technology, there's no denying its ability to improve our lives in countless ways. From automation to smarter work processes, technology offers many possibilities that can make life more convenient and carefree. However, it's important to remember that technology needs to work for us, not against us. One great way to ensure a healthy technology-life balance is to set aside specific time slots where you disconnect entirely. This freedom from constant connectivity can offer a great sense of relief and enable you to truly be present at the moment. So, while technology has many advantages, allow yourself to unplug and recharge.

Great Tools For Increasing Work-Life Balance

If you want a more balanced and happy life, start by assessing how you currently manage your professional and personal commitments. Taking small steps toward a better work-life balance can significantly impact your health, happiness, and productivity. For example, consider making time for exercise, family and friends, and hobbies outside of work. Additionally, try setting boundaries at work, such as not checking your email after a certain time or delegating tasks where possible. By finding ways to prioritize both your professional and personal life, you'll be better equipped to lead a fulfilling and satisfying life.

Here are some other pro tips for finding a better work-life balance.

Let go

Are you constantly striving for perfection at work? It's understandable to want to do your best and impress those around you, but sometimes taking on too much responsibility can lead to unnecessary stress. Remember, it's okay to let go and not constantly chase after flawlessness. This constant pursuit of perfection can result in an endless cycle of higher expectations, leaving you unsatisfied. Don't let the pressure get to you - give yourself some grace and focus on doing your best without obsessing over every little detail.

◼ Prioritize Your Mental Health

You may have heard that meditation is a powerful tool for unplugging and rebalancing yourself after a long day at work, and it's true! Utilizing techniques like breathing exercises and mindfulness can enhance the effects of your meditation. Plus, you don't have to wait until the end of the day to benefit from it - taking just five minutes during your workday to focus solely on your breathing can work wonders. It's a simple yet powerful way to increase focus and reduce stress. So next time you feel overwhelmed, take a moment to unplug and practice meditation for a balanced and rejuvenated mind.

◼ What About Some Helpful Planner Tools & Apps?

As a busy professional, you know the struggle of balancing work and life demands. Fortunately, there are effective strategies you can implement better to organize your time, tasks, and team members, leading to a happier and more productive work-life balance. In addition, by taking advantage of tools designed to boost efficiency and productivity, you can free up your time and space for the things that matter to you.

Here are some of our favorite apps for work-life balance:

Rescue Time

Imagine having a personal productivity assistant that tailors its approach to fit your unique work style and schedule. Rescue Time is the ultimate time management tool that helps you accomplish more while reducing the stress of a chaotic workday. With Rescue Time, you can set personalized goals and watch your productivity skyrocket, leaving you with more time to focus on what matters. Say goodbye to wasted hours and hello to a more peaceful work life with Rescue Time.

Cozi

Meet your new best friend for controlling your family's schedule and tasks: Cozi. This handy tool helps you and your family easily create and share a grocery list and manage schedules for school and extracurricular activities with anyone who has the app. In just a few clicks, you can simplify your busy life and focus on what really matters - quality time with your loved ones.

Conclusion

Congratulations on reaching the end of this ebook! You now clearly understand what work-life balance truly means and how to achieve it. It's time to put what you've learned into action by implementing the ultimate work-life balance checklist. Remember, finding balance is an ongoing process that requires dedication and commitment. Don't be discouraged if you stumble along the way. Instead, use the checklist as a guide to help you stay on track and adjust as needed.

Additionally, it's important to prioritize self-care and make time for the things that bring you joy outside of work. By doing so, you'll not only improve your well-being but also increase your productivity and overall job satisfaction. Here's to achieving a true work-life balance!

www.ingramcontent.com/pod-product-compliance
Lightning Source LLC
Chambersburg PA
CBHW070454130626
46553CB00006B/2411